Amazing Planet Earth

THE WORLD'S OCEANS

JEN GREEN

SAUNDERS
BOOK COMPANY

Published by Saunders Book Company
27 Stewart Road
Collingwood, ON Canada L9Y 4M7

Printed in the United States of America

Library of Congress Cataloging-in-Publication Data

Green, Jen.
  The world's oceans / Jen Green.
      p. cm. -- (Amazing planet earth)
  Includes index.
  ISBN 978-1-897563-81-6 (pbk)
  1. Ocean--Juvenile literature. I. Title.
  GC21.5.G77 2010
  551.46--dc22

                          2008055500

Created by Q2AMedia
Editor: Michael Downey
Art Director: Rahul Dhiman
Designers: Harleen Mehta, Ritu Chopra
Picture Researcher: Shreya Sharma
Line Artist: Sibi N. Devasia
Coloring Artists: Aadil Ahmad, Ajay Luthra, Mahender Kumar

All words in **bold** can be found in the glossary on pages 30–31.

Web site information is correct at time of going to press. However, the publishers cannot
accept liability for any information or links found on third-party Web sites.

Picture credits
t=top b=bottom c=center l=left r=right
Cover Image: Mana Photo/ Shutterstock.
Back Cover Image: Walt Stepanski/ BigStockPhoto

Insides: Phooey/ iStockphoto: Title Page, Neil Farrin/ Jai/ Corbis: 4,Mollypix/ Shutterstock: 4-5, NASA: 6, Nik Taylor / Alamy: 7,
Phooey/ iStockphoto: 9, Index Stock Imagery/ Photolibrary: 10, Jill Lang\ Shutterstock: 10-11, Arctic-Images Arctic-Images/ Flirt
Collection/ Photolibrary: 14, Ragnar Th. Sigurdsson/ Photographers Direct: 15, lloyd s clements/ Shutterstock: 16-17, Pieckas/
Dreamstime: 17, Bullit Marquez/Associated Press: 19, Benjamin Lowy/ Corbis: 20, NOAA: 21, NASA: 22, Ray Fairall/ Associated
Press: 23, NOAA: 25, Tomassino/ iStockphoto: 26, FelixStrummer/ iStockphoto: 27, Benelux/ zefa/ Corbis: 28, Bettmann/ Corbis: 29,
lloyd s clements/ Shutterstock: 31,

Q2AMedia Art Bank: 6, 8, 12, 13, 18, 24.

9 8 7 6 5 4 3 2 1

Contents

Five Oceans

More than two-thirds of Earth's surface is covered by salty seas and oceans. Less than one-third is made up of dry land. The world's vast, deep oceans still contain many secrets waiting to be discovered.

Deep Blue World

Earth appears blue when seen from space because so much of it is covered by water in five great oceans. This water reflects blue light shining down from the sky. Earth's five oceans are the Pacific Ocean, Atlantic Ocean, Indian Ocean, Arctic Ocean, and the stormy Southern Ocean that surrounds Antarctica in the southern hemisphere.

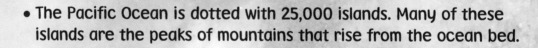

• The Pacific Ocean is dotted with 25,000 islands. Many of these islands are the peaks of mountains that rise from the ocean bed.

• Ocean water is made salty by the minerals that are carried into the oceans by rivers.

DATA FILE

- - - - - - - - - - - - - - - -

- A sea is an area of water partly or totally enclosed by land. An ocean is a much larger expanse of water without boundaries.

- The Pacific is the largest ocean at about 65 million square miles (170 million sq km) or one-third of Earth's surface. The average depth is 14,000 feet (4,200 m). It is the world's deepest ocean.

- The smallest and shallowest ocean is the Arctic Ocean. It covers an area of 5 million square miles (14 million sq km). Its surface is mostly frozen.

Moving in Circles

Waves move ocean water around all the time. Most ocean waves are started by winds that sweep across the water's surface. As waves roll across the ocean, the water spins in a circle. That is why seabirds bob up and down in the same place rather than being swept across the surface. In shallow waters, the seabed blocks this circular motion. This creates white crests as waves break on the water's surface.

Rising and Sinking

Surface **currents** are also caused by winds. These currents flow in giant circles called **gyres**. Alongside these, there are other, deeper ocean currents that flow in the opposite direction, as well as places where water rises and sinks.

Currents and Tides

Currents are giant underwater rivers that move through the world's vast oceans. These currents can be warm or cold and have a powerful effect on temperatures on Earth.

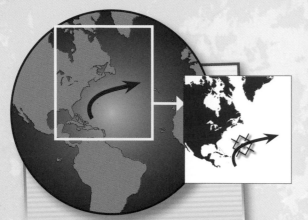

Feature: Gulf Stream/North Atlantic Current
Location: North Atlantic
Width: 53–93 mi (85–150 km)
Depth: 2,625–4,000 feet (800–1,200 m)

Giant Warming Current

Starting in the Gulf of Mexico, the Gulf Stream Current flows north through the Atlantic Ocean, warming the east coast of North America. The Gulf Stream is called the North Atlantic Current as it continues northeast toward Europe. In winter, the Gulf Stream is up to 23.4°F (13°C) warmer than the waters around it.

• The warm Gulf Stream flows through the Atlantic Ocean along the coast of North America toward Europe.

World's Highest Tides

The North Atlantic Current warms the shores of western Britain and the Severn Estuary. This estuary marks the point where Britain's longest river, the River Severn, drains into the Bristol Channel and then out into the Atlantic Ocean. The coastline of the Severn Estuary is washed by some of the world's highest tides that rise and fall by up to 50 feet (15 m).

Effect of the Moon

Tides are changes in sea level brought about by the Moon. The Moon's **gravity** pulls the ocean toward it, causing a huge mass of water to collect in one place in the ocean. As Earth spins around, the mass of water moves across the oceans, forming a high tide where it rises against coasts. The difference between low and high tide is called the tidal range.

DATA FILE

- The Bay of Fundy in eastern Canada has the biggest tidal range. The difference between high and low tide can be up to 56 feet (17 m).

- The Sun's gravity also affects the world's tides. At a certain time each month, the Sun and Moon line up so that their pulls combine. This produces a very high tide.

• At low tide, the sea drains out of England's Severn Estuary, leaving boats stranded on the mud.

Shaping the Seashore

The coast is where the land meets the sea. There are over 310,000 miles (500,000 km) of coasts around the edges of the world's continents and islands.

Collapsing Cliffs

On every coast around the world, night and day, waves lap or crash against the shoreline. When powerful waves hit the shore at high tide, they can hurl rocks and pebbles against coastal cliffs. This slowly wears away the cliff in a process called **erosion**. In time, waves can damage the bottom of a cliff, causing huge chunks of the cliff to collapse into the sea.

• Ocean waves carve seashore features such as stacks, arches, and caves.

Headland

Stack

Arch

Cave

Craggy Headlands

On coasts, soft rocks such as chalk wear away more quickly than hard rocks such as **granite**. Areas of soft rock can erode to form wide **bays**, while hard rocks are shaped into craggy headlands. But pounding waves can gradually carve caves in even the toughest of rocks. If two caves are on either side of a headland, they can wear through to form an arch. When the arch collapses, it leaves a pillar in the sea called a **stack**.

News Flash

June 1993

A huge landslide on Britain's east coast has sent a hotel tumbling into the sea. Scarborough's Holbeck Hall Hotel was built in the 1880s. On June 3, it began to slide toward the sea after rain weakened the cliff edge. On June 7, the cliff gave way completely, and the building crashed onto the beach.

Beaches and Spits

Along some stretches of coast, the ocean creates new land. This happens because ocean currents carry rocky **fragments** and fine sand. When the current slows in sheltered places, such as bays, waves drop the sand and stones. This makes a beach. Sometimes, a long finger of land forms and stretches out to sea. This is called a **spit**.

• The Twelve Apostles are sea stacks off the Australian coast.

Sand Islands

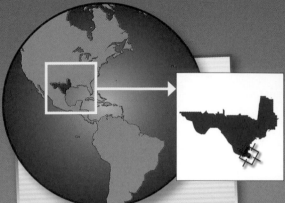

Feature: Padre Island
Location: Southern U.S.
Length: 125 mi (200 km)
Speciality: The longest barrier island in the world

• Padre Island is famous for its sandy beaches.

Over thousands of years, sandy deposits can build up offshore to form long, thin islands. These formations of sand islands have occured on long stretches of coast in the United States.

Slowly Moving Island

Islands made from sand dropped by the sea are called **barrier islands**. These islands protect the **mainland** from stormy seas. The world's longest barrier island is Padre Island in the Gulf of Mexico off the southern coast of Texas. Padre Island began forming 4,500 years ago and is now 125 miles (200 km) long. The constant action of the sea slowly moves it toward the mainland.

Galveston Totally Destroyed

Coastal landscapes never stay the same. Change happens the fastest during storms when huge waves lash and pound the shoreline. Sometimes, entire islands can shift sideways or even be swept away altogether. During a storm in 1900, huge waves swept over the town of Galveston in southern Texas. Built on a barrier island, Galveston was destroyed.

Saved from Collapsing

Coastal buildings may need to be rescued when their sandy foundations are attacked by the sea. The Cape Hatteras lighthouse was in danger of collapsing. Built in the 1870s on a sandy barrier island in the southeastern United States, the lighthouse was moved 0.6 miles (1 km) inland to a safer place in 1999.

• Cape Hatteras lighthouse now stands on safer ground having been rescued from the sea's pounding waves.

DATA FILE

• The Atlantic coast of North America has one of the world's longest chains of barrier islands. Some 300 islands stretch from Maine in the north to Mexico in the south.

• In 1992, a **hurricane** shifted the barrier island Isles Dernieres In the southeastern United States toward the shore.

Ocean Bed

The world's ocean floors have dramatic, hidden scenery. Beyond the shallow areas called continental shelves, which are about 50 miles (80 km) wide, the ocean floor drops steeply to its inky-black depths.

Huge Ocean Trenches

The beds of Earth's great oceans are covered by giant **plains** that stretch hundreds of miles. In places, these flat areas are broken by sheer cliffs and huge trenches. The depth of some trenches is greater than the height of the world's highest mountains. Long chains of undersea mountains and single peaks are also found in the oceans. Some of these mountains are active volcanoes that shoot out red-hot **lava**.

• The craggy scenery on the ocean bed

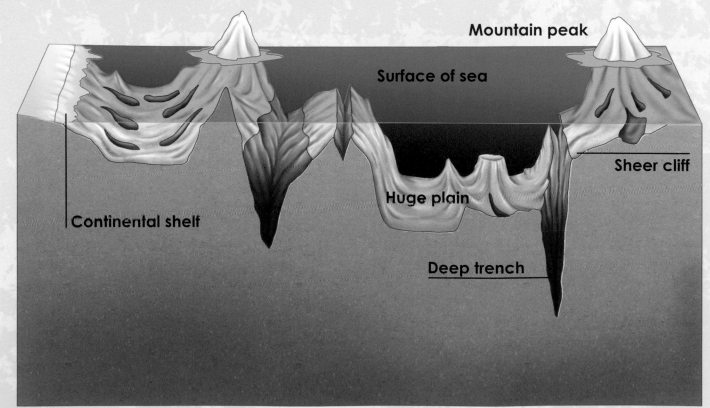

Mountain peak

Surface of sea

Sheer cliff

Huge plain

Continental shelf

Deep trench

Crashing Plates

Mountains, volcanoes, and trenches are formed by the movement of the huge sections of rock that make up Earth's crust, or outer layer. These rocky sections, called tectonic plates, float on hot, liquid rock below the crust and drift very slowly. These plates can crash into each other or move apart.

Masses of Lava

When one plate is pushed below another plate on the ocean bed, a deep trench is formed. Where two plates pull apart, hot lava rises up to fill the gap and form what is known as a rift valley. Over time, huge quantities of lava can build up to create a high mountain ridge.

News Flash

December 1977

Scientists exploring the Pacific Ocean in a **submersible** have made a startling discovery. Deep underwater, they have found tall chimneys spouting black clouds of hot, mineral-rich water. Scientists believe these black smokers form on volcanic ridges where tectonic plates are moving apart.

• Earth's massive tectonic plates fit together like an enormous jigsaw puzzle.

NORTH AMERICAN PLATE

EURASIAN PLATE

PACIFIC PLATE

PACIFIC PLATE

AFRICAN PLATE

INDIAN PLATE

SOUTH AMERICAN PLATE

NAZCA PLATE

AUSTRALIAN PLATE

ANTARCTIC PLATE

Volcanic Ridge

A long chain of undersea mountains called the Mid-Atlantic Ridge runs north to south down the center of the Atlantic Ocean. This ridge stretches from Iceland to the Southern Ocean.

Ever-Widening Ocean

The Atlantic Ocean has been forming over millions of years. It is still getting wider by about 0.8 inches (2 cm) a year. Originally, there was no ocean. The huge hollow for the ocean, which later filled with water, gradually formed as some of Earth's continents were pushed apart by volcanic activity. These volcanoes also formed the mountains of the Mid-Atlantic Ridge.

• Undersea volcanoes spill out red-hot lava along parts of the Mid-Atlantic Ridge.

Feature: Mid-Atlantic Ridge
Location: Runs the length of the Atlantic Ocean
Length: 7,020 mi (11,300 km)

Creation of Iceland

Many of the massive mountains that make up the Mid-Atlantic Ridge rise 13,125 feet (4,000 m) above the sea floor. In most places, the tops of these mountains are about 8,200 feet (2,500 m) below the surface of the Atlantic Ocean. But in other regions, so much lava has built up that an island has formed. Iceland is an island that has formed in this way. Iceland is made up of a dark rock called basalt that forms when red-hot lava spills out of a volcano and is cooled quickly by sea water. Today, there is still plenty of volcanic activity on Iceland and in the nearby ocean bed.

- In 1963, the volcanic island of Surtsey was formed in the North Atlantic.

News Flash

November 1963

A new island has appeared in the icy North Atlantic. On November 15, 1963, fishermen watched as a pillar of black smoke rose from the ocean. Lava soon broke the surface to form an island, which has been named Surtsey after the Icelandic god of fire.

Dangerous Waters

The world's oceans hold many perils—for ships and people living on the coast. Powerful waves and hidden rocks can smash and sink ships, while violent storms can rip through coastal towns.

Terrifying Waters

Most sailors have experienced the truly terrifying power of the sea. Sudden and violent storms can cause extremely rough seas. Lashing winds are whipped up, and surging, crashing waves smash onto ships and batter exposed coasts. These conditions are especially deadly for small sailing vessels. When caught in the middle of a storm, these boats are helpless against the raging sea.

- The bright beams of lighthouses warn ships away from jagged rocks at night.

Jagged Rocks

Scientists think that there could be as many as 3 million ships lying at the bottom of the world's seas and oceans. Most of them were sunk by the jagged rocks and sandbanks that lie hidden under the water's surface. When a ship's captain has to navigate through fog, things can become even more dangerous. Sometimes, ships collide when sailing through thick fog.

News Flash
February 6, 1933

The U.S. ship *Ramapo* has been caught in a violent storm in the Pacific as it sailed home to the United States from the Philippines. The crew reported waves up to 112 feet (34 m) high, the highest ever recorded.

Underwater Hazards

What can be done to help guard against these dangers? Lighthouses and buoys play an important part in warning ships of nearby reefs and other perils. Ships are now also equipped with **sonar** devices that detect underwater hazards. Modern **navigation** equipment and accurate weather reports help ships to steer a safe course through even the most dangerous conditions.

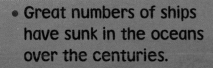

- Great numbers of ships have sunk in the oceans over the centuries.

Deadly Tsunamis

Undersea volcanic explosions and earthquakes can cause giant waves called tsunamis. These killer waves can travel across oceans for thousands of miles.

Waves Sweeping Ashore

On December 26, 2004, a powerful earthquake struck off the coast of Indonesia. This caused tsunamis to form in all directions from the earthquake's center, called its epicenter. Giant waves hit the Aceh region of northern Sumatra just 15 minutes later. In 90 minutes, it reached Thailand and Malaysia where tourists witnessed a terrifying sight. First the sea drained away from beaches, then huge waves rolled in and swept ashore.

• In 2004, tsunamis spread out across the Indian Ocean from the earthquake zone.

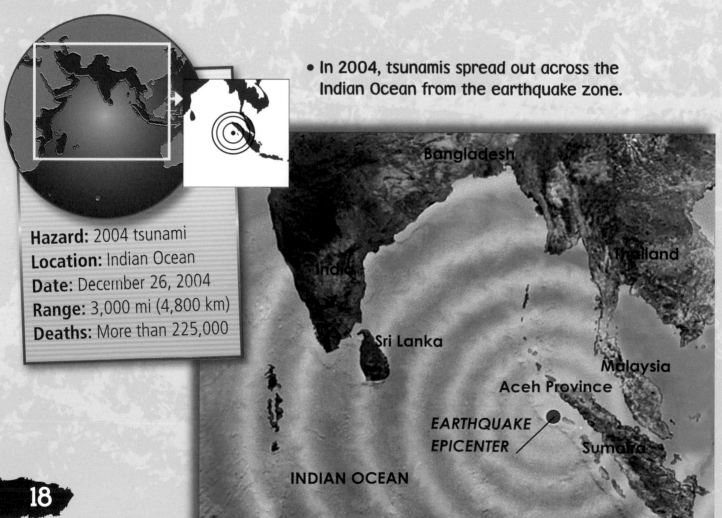

Hazard: 2004 tsunami
Location: Indian Ocean
Date: December 26, 2004
Range: 3,000 mi (4,800 km)
Deaths: More than 225,000

Bangladesh

Thailand

India

Sri Lanka

Malaysia

Aceh Province

EARTHQUAKE EPICENTER

Sumatra

INDIAN OCEAN

• Over 130,000 people died in the city of Banda Aceh in Sumatra after the earthquake and tsunami.

Water Rearing Up

In the open ocean, tsunamis are low waves about 3.3 feet (1 m) high. They travel at hundreds of miles per hour. It is only when they reach shore that they slow down and become much higher. In 2004, it took 2 hours after the earthquake struck for tsunami waves to reach Sri Lanka and southern India. People, animals, and even vehicles were swept along by the swirling water. About 7 hours after the earthquake, the tsunamis had reached Africa, 3,000 miles (4,800 km) away.

News Flash

December 26, 2004

Coasts around the Indian Ocean have been hit by tsunamis following a major earthquake on the seabed. Over 200,000 people are feared dead. The Indonesian city of Banda Aceh has suffered the worst damage. This is the worst natural disaster of the early twenty-first century.

Millions Made Homeless

The day after the Indian Ocean tsunamis, the damage that the disaster had caused became clear for the whole world to see. Towns and villages all around the Indian Ocean were destroyed, and millions of people had lost their homes. The island of Sumatra was devasted. The tragedy brought death and destruction to Thailand where many fishing boats were wrecked and **crops** were ruined. In Sri Lanka, to the west, about 1,500 people died. Even further west, in Somalia, Africa, more than 300 people were killed.

• After the 2004 tsunami disaster, relief workers used elephants to move debris.

Looking for Survivors

Countries around the world sent food, medicines, tents for shelter, and rescue workers to the disaster region. The first task was to search ruined buildings for any survivors. After this, the work of clearing the debris began so that people could start to rebuild their shattered lives.

Sounding the Alarm

A tsunami warning system is now being set up in the Indian Ocean. A similar system already exists in the Pacific Ocean. Sensors on the seabed warn of earthquakes and volcanic **eruptions** that can trigger tsunamis. If the alarm is given, people know to go as quickly as possible to higher ground for safety.

• This buoy marks the site of an earthquake sensor on the seabed. It is part of a tsunami warning system.

DATA FILE

- The word tsunami means "harbor wave" in Japanese.

- Tsunamis are hardly noticed out at sea. They build up as they reach harbors and coasts.

- In 1896, the Japanese island of Honshu was wrecked by tsunamis, and 28,000 people died. Fishermen working out in the sea barely noticed the waves that passed under their fishing boats.

- In 1964, an earthquake in Alaska set off tsunamis that swelled to a height of 40 feet (12 m). These are still among the highest ever recorded.

Storm Surges

High seas called storm surges can be whipped up by storms and hurricanes. In 1992, a violent hurricane named Andrew produced a storm surge that battered Florida.

Heavy Floods

Hurricanes are very powerful storms that develop over warm seas in summer. Winds spin around a column of calm air in the center, called the eye. These winds whirl at up to 200 miles (320 km) per hour and draw up water from the ocean. The water that piles up below the eye is the **storm surge**. When the hurricane hits land, the storm surge acts like a very high tide and can cause floods and massive destruction.

• An aerial photograph of Hurricane Andrew whirling close to Florida.

Trail of Destruction

In August 1992, Hurricane Andrew brought with it a storm surge 16 feet (5 m) high. Swirling water and high winds picked up trucks, boats, and even aircraft and tossed them further inland. The hurricane raged across the tip of Florida, leaving a trail of destruction about 25 miles (40 km) wide. One of the most destructive storms of the twentieth century, Hurricane Andrew caused an amazing $26 billion in damage.

• The violent power of Hurricane Andrew in 1992 devastated many towns in Florida.

DATA FILE

- Hurricanes and storm surges have caused great destruction in low-lying Bangladesh on the shores of the Indian Ocean. In 1970, a hurricane caused widespread flooding, and 500,000 people died.

- Hurricanes are known as typhoons in the Pacific. In the Indian Ocean, they are called cyclones.

- In 2005, Hurricane Katrina flooded the city of New Orleans in Louisiana. More than 1,800 people died.

Giant Icebergs

Ice is a major hazard in waters around the North and South poles. In the north, icebergs drift south from the Arctic and are dangerous to ships in the North Atlantic.

Mass of Hidden Ice

Icebergs are huge chunks of ice that break off glaciers in Earth's **polar regions**. Less than one-fifth of an iceberg shows above the water's surface, the rest is underwater. That is why it is so dangerous for ships to approach these floating masses of ice.

Hazard: Iceberg
Location: North Atlantic
Incident: Sinking of the TItanic
Date: April 15, 1912
Deaths: 1,490

• The *Titanic* was supposed to be unsinkable, but it dropped to the bottom of the Atlantic Ocean when it hit an iceberg.

Tragedy Strikes

The *Titanic* was one of the largest, most luxurious ships ever built. It was just four days into its first voyage from Britain to New York in April 1912 when it struck an iceberg. The **liner** sank in less than 3 hours, and 1,490 passengers and crew drowned. Only 700 people, mostly women and children, escaped in lifeboats.

Wreck Discovered

For 70 years, the *Titanic* lay hidden on the bed of the Atlantic Ocean. In 1985, a diving team found the wreck below the surface. Shortly after, a small U.S. Navy submersible, the *Alvin*, was sent down to look over the wreck. Later, many objects were recovered from the ship.

Deep-Sea creatures

Alvin is the world's most famous submersible. In 1977, scientists in *Alvin* discovered the first black smokers that form in volcanic ridges in the ocean. *Alvin* has also been used to bring deep-sea creatures to the surface. Just 23 feet (7 m) long, *Alvin* carries three people.

- The submersible *Alvin* has made many important discoveries in the ocean depths.

News Flash

April 15, 1912

The liner *Titanic* has met with disaster in the North Atlantic. The crew radioed for help shortly after midnight on April 15 after hitting an iceberg, but sank two hours later. Rescue ships arrived in time to pick up survivors in lifeboats, but more than 1,400 souls went down with the ship.

Rising Seas

Today, sea levels are rising and the polar ice caps are getting smaller. In the future, this may lead to severe flooding in coastal areas.

Melting Ice

During long, cold periods called **Ice Ages**, ice covered much of the land. Sea levels were lower because so much water was frozen on land. During the last Ice Age, which ended about 10,000 years ago, sea levels were 295 feet (90 m) lower than today. When the **climate** warmed, the ice melted, and the sea flooded coastal valleys. This formed steep-sided inlets called **fjords** on some coasts.

- Fjords are steep-sided inlets. These form when the sea floods a coastal valley.

Earth Heating Up

The world is slowly becoming warmer because some gases in the atmosphere are trapping the Sun's heat close to Earth. Scientists call this **global warming**. The gases are produced when we burn **fossil fuels**, such as oil and coal, in our power plants, factories, homes, and cars.

Danger of Flooding

Ice in the polar regions has started to melt because of global warming. As the oceans expand and the water levels rise, more and more low-lying islands and coastal cities will be put in danger of flooding.

- Rising seas could flood these low-lying islands in the Indian Ocean.

DATA FILE

- World temperatures rose by about .9°F (0.5°C) in the 1900s. They went up fastest in the polar regions.

- Temperatures may rise by 3.6–7.2°F (2–4°C) by the year 2100.

- A rise of 7.2°F (4°C) would melt ice in the polar regions, increasing the risk of flooding.

- In the late 1990s, a huge chunk of ice broke off an ice shelf in Antarctica and floated away. Ice frequently breaks off, but this was the largest chunk so far.

- Sea levels have risen by 6–8 inches (15–20 cm) in the last 100 years due to melting polar ice caps.

Threatened Coast

Hazard: Rising sea levels
Location: The Netherlands
Area: 15,768 sq mi
(40,840 sq km) of which
19 percent is reclaimed land
Flood-prone areas:
Reclaimed coastal land

The Netherlands is one of the lowest-lying countries in the world. It has been hit by floods many times in its history. Now it is threatened by rising sea levels due to global warming.

Reclaiming Land

The Dutch have been reclaiming land from the sea for centuries. High walls called **dikes** have been built on coasts to keep the North Sea from flooding land. Water is pumped out of the marshy ground behind the dikes to create fields called **polders**.

• These pillars, part of the flood defenses in the Netherlands, protect the land from the sea.

Repairing the Dikes

Low-lying parts of the Netherlands have flooded many times. In 1953, a violent storm caused a storm surge in the North Sea. Water broke through the dikes and flooded up to 775 square miles (2,000 sq km) of land. When the sea retreated, the damaged dikes took months to repair. After this, the Dutch built a network of flood barriers to protect their country from the destructive power of the sea.

• In 1953, flooding caused by a storm surge left many towns in the Netherlands damaged. Cold temperatures made the situation worse for many of the victims of the floods.

Safeguarding Coasts

What can be done to protect low-lying countries from the growing danger of flooding caused by global warming? Most scientists believe that the first, and most urgent, step we can take is to use much less oil and coal, which damage the atmosphere. Instead, there should be a great effort around the world to switch to using other types of fuels and energies that produce less pollution.

News Flash

February 2, 1953

The Netherlands and eastern England have been hit by floods after a severe storm. Winds of 71 miles (115 km) per hour piled sea water into the narrow channel of the North Sea. Over 80 dikes have collapsed in Holland, and 1,800 people are feared dead.

Glossary

barrier island an island made of sand that has been deposited by the sea

bay a curving inlet on the coast

black smoker an undersea volcano that spouts clouds of hot, dark, mineral-rich water

climate the long-term weather pattern of a region

crops plants that are grown each year to feed people and animals

current a regular flow of water in a certain direction

dike a bank built to prevent flooding by a river or the sea

erosion the wearing away of rocks by water, wind, or ice

eruption when a volcano becomes active and gives off ash, gas, and lava

fjord a steep-sided inlet formed when the sea floods a deep valley by the coast

fossil fuel a fuel that is formed in Earth's crust

fragment a small piece

global warming a general rise in temperatures caused by a buildup of gases in the air that trap the Sun's heat

granite a very tough rock often used in the construction of buildings

gravity the pulling power of the Earth, Moon, Sun, or another huge object in space

gyre a huge circular ocean current

hurricane a large, powerful spinning storm that is also called a cyclone or a typhoon

Ice Age a long, cold period in our planet's history during which ice covered more of Earth's surface than it does now

lava hot, melted rock from underground that surges up to the surface when a volcano erupts

liner a large and luxurious passenger ship that sails regularly between specific ports

mainland the main area of a country and does not include any islands that may also form part of that country

navigation the guiding of ships from one place to another

plain a large area of land that is flat

polar regions areas at or around the North and South poles

polder a field made from reclaimed land

sonar a device that uses sound waves to find objects underwater

spit a sandy finger of land stretching out to sea

stack a pillar of rock standing in the sea

storm surge a mound of water whipped up by a storm or hurricane

submersible an underwater craft

Index

Web Sites

www.kidsgeo.com/geography-for-kids/0134-the-earths-oceans.php
This site describes the four oceans as well as tides, currents, and ice.

www.fema.gov/hazard/tsunami
This site provides information about tsunamis and what to do if a tsunami threatens your area.

http://aquarium.ucsd.edu/Education/Learning_Resources/Voyager_for_Kids/ earth_puzzle/
This site looks at the basics of plate tectonics.

http://www.fema.gov/kids/hurr.htm
This site for kids provides facts about hurricanes.